GOING SOLO

ONE-ACT PLAYS FOR ONE ACTOR

ANDREW BISS

Original cover images © Wisky

Cover design by Ernest Waggenheim

First Printing, 2017

All rights reserved

ISBN-13: 978-1547298976
ISBN-10: 1547298979

ENTR'ACTE
EDITIONS

"It is the confession, not the priest, that gives us absolution."

~Oscar Wilde

CONTENTS

BIG GIRL

BIG GIRL

An overweight young woman named Peggy appraises her recently purchased self-help book, "The Bigger the Better."

CHARACTER

PEGGY: Significantly overweight. Smart, independent-
           minded, with a caustic edge. Early 20s.

SETTING & TIME

SETTING: Unspecified.

TIME: The present.

Big Girl premiered in New York at the Times Square Arts Center in 2008, produced by 3Graces Theater Company and directed by Kathleen Bishop.

Peggy..Kelli Lynn Harrison

At Rise: A spotlight reveals PEGGY, an overweight young woman in her early-twenties, standing centre stage holding a book in her hands. PEGGY stares out at the audience with a proud, intrepid expression on her face.

PEGGY: (*In a defiant announcement.*) I weigh 276 pounds and I love every single God-given one of them!
    (*Pause.*)
I don't, actually. Not if I were being honest. But that's what you're supposed to repeat, according to the instructions in the book.
    (*Beat.*)
It's called, "The Bigger the Better." Written by…
    (*Beat.*)
Oh…isn't that odd. I can't recall her name. Ordinarily, I could quote you from here to eternity on just about anyone, but at this precise moment I'm drawing a complete blank on the author. An American, I think. (*Squinting at the book cover.*) Should have brought my glasses. (*Holding the book before her.*) It's meant to empower you, apparently – repeating this mantra. They suggest standing completely naked in front of a full-length mirror under overhead lighting and repeating at least twenty times before going to bed, "I weigh 276 pounds and I love every single God-given one of them." Not that it says "276" of course. It just leaves a blank space for you to plop in whatever it is you're lugging around. Then you're supposed to wake up the next morning feeling completely at peace with your physical being and the world in which it moves…or lumbers…or words to that effect. Whatever the case, it's not working. I'm not sure if it's because I hate my body or because I don't believe in God…though I suspect the latter. At any rate, I've a feeling I was had.
    (*Beat.*)
As Nietzsche so adroitly put it, "Does wisdom perhaps appear on the earth as a raven which is inspired by the smell of carrion?"
    (*Beat.*)

Perhaps yes, perhaps no. But I did buy the book.

(*Beat.*)

Maybe I'll write a book someday. I'd title it: "How to Hate Your Bloated Carcass, Yet Still Continue to Enjoy a Relatively Happy, Healthy and Productive Life…Barring One or Two Exceptions…Especially When Sitting Alone on a Saturday Night with a Bottle of Vodka and a Bellyful of Bile." Or something like that.

(*Beat.*)

I think I'd need an editor.

(*Pause.*)

I've always been big. I was born big. I was a big baby. Still am in some respects. In fact, one of the earliest memories I have is of my Aunt Nester staring down at me, her thin lips contorted into a forced expression of adoration, saying to my mother, "My word, you've got a big girl there, haven't you, Georgie."

(*Beat.*)

She's dead now. Not my mother – my Aunt Nester. A severe stroke whilst pruning her beloved roses in her front garden. She fell into them face first, the thorns of her pride and joy gashing open her wizened face in her moment of need. They did a good job, though – at the mortuary, that is. She looked quite regal, all dished up and served before us, there in her casket. I stared hard at her face but I couldn't see even the trace of a scar. Mum fell apart. Sadly, all I felt was a slight twinge of guilt as I contorted my not-so-thin lips into a forced expression of loss.

(*Beat.*)

And so it goes.

(*Pause.*)

I think self-hatred is vastly underrated, don't you? I mean, everyone seems to have such a negative view of it. But if you really think about it, it makes life so much easier in so many ways. For a start, you don't have to bother giving yourself all those tiresome confidence-building pep talks inside your head every time you look in the mirror or step outside the front door. You can simply hate what you see before you, shrug your shoulders and get on with your business. And if someone insults you or shoots you a disdainful glare, it doesn't sting or chip away at your delicately crafted shell of self-confidence – it just lands harmlessly in that boggy pit of everything you already despise and fizzles out with barely a flicker. You don't wrestle with it, you just absorb it. It can save an awful lot of time in this fast-paced world of ours. Think about it.

(*Pause.*)

"It's not what you look at that matters, it's what you see." That's according to Henry David Thoreau, and he'd have been quite surprised at what people see had he been me. When you're the size I am you become an object, a thing – not a person. People who might, in any other circumstances, be perfectly polite and well-mannered, somehow feel entirely comfortable staring at me in the most blatant, obvious way. They don't see me, of course, they see a mass – a misshapen mass; never imagining for a moment that there might be someone living inside it...looking back. I become an object of curiosity. They look away self-consciously when a person in a wheelchair approaches, but with me it's open season. Some simply gawp, slack jawed. Others eye me more studiously, as if taking mental notes on the nature of this strange, deformed specimen they've just stumbled upon. Others, as I said before, spit looks of disdain or disgust, as if I were the living embodiment of the sins of overindulgence, and should, at my earliest opportunity, carve off large chunks of my flesh and mail them to malnourished children in developing countries.

(*Beat.*)

Wonder what I'd taste like? Sweet and sour is my guess. Probably go down a treat with some white rice and a Tsingtao. I could be big in China without even going there. Well, bits of me would be there, I suppose. And as Confucius so discouragingly pointed out,

"No matter where you go, there you are."

(*Pause.*)

According to "The Bigger the Better," we all belong to one of three groups: endomorphs, whose metabolisms require a far greater amount of effort in order to lose weight; ectomorphs, who have the opposite problem; and mesomorphs, who can pretty much lose it or gain it at will – think Robert De Niro in "Raging Bull." Thus, they say, as an endomorph, you should stop punishing yourself with the guilt and shame thrust upon you by the vacuous standards of an image-obsessed culture and begin loving and respecting the body you were given by Mother Nature. Or, in other words, tell Marie Claire to kiss your fat, flabby, cellulite-riddled ass.

(*Beat.*)

I have only one problem with this theory – I want to be Marie Claire. Well, maybe not Marie Claire herself – she's probably ninety-years-old by now, with mummified silicon tits and a face in perpetual G-force. But I'd kill to be one of those people…to be one of those bodies…one of them. (*Becoming agitated.*) Telling yourself you like the way you look is easy. Believing it is an entirely different kettle of whales. That's because, if I were being honest, I'm tired. I'm tired of feeling out of breath all the time; I'm tired of people looking through me not at me; I'm sick to death of buying crap clothes from "specialty" stores, or from mail-order companies whose crap clothes never fit right anyway. I want to look chic. I want to look sexy. I want to feel sexy. I want to take my clothes off and not feel ashamed of my body the next time I go home with some drunk-off-his-head asshole who didn't get the girl he was chasing all night. Just for once in my life I'd like not to feel like the commiserating blowjob at the end of a disappointing evening.

(*In a masculine voice.*)

"Then lose some weight, ya fat bitch!"

(*Beat.*)

No shit, ya dumb fuck!

(In a masculine voice.)

"Ooh, Piggy's pissed!"

(Beat.)

Peggy isn't pissed; Peggy's up-to-fucking-here with fucks like you that perpetuate the specie with more dumb fucks with the same fat heads, the same small dicks, the same inability of independent thought, and the same brainless look in their eyes. That's what Peggy's sick of.

(In a masculine voice.)

"Oh, then fuck you, Miss Piggy. You need to lighten up – startin' with ya gut."

(Beat.)

Yeah, fuck off – go – get outta here! I don't give a crap! I don't need your shit…I don't need you. I'm a big girl now…see?

(Beat.)

I can take it…all of it.

(Pause, then quietly to herself.)

I'm a big girl.

(Pause.)

I don't have enough friends, according to my mother. "Peggy, you don't get out enough – mix, mingle – you've got ever such a pretty face." God, how I hate it when she says that; as if it were some sort of consolation prize for a contestant who didn't make the grade on a game show. And it is a game, that much I do know. Anyway, I don't like going out much – it's usually more trouble than it's worth. "No vale la pena," as the Spanish say. And the question of friends is even deadlier. If I'm with other fatties I'm less self-conscious on one level, but on another I feel like a female-in-heat amongst a herd of roaming buffalo. On the other hand, whenever I hang out with skinny girls, I either get the feeling from some that I'm only there because they feel sorry for me, or from others – haunted by the fact that they gained 5lbs last month – are desperate to look skinny by comparison, like in some rigged taste test. Needless to say, it's always me that fails the Pepsi Challenge.

(*Pause.*)

If negative feelings can eat you up inside, then I, by rights – and as you may have already speculated – should resemble something not too dissimilar from Karen Carpenter in her latter stages by this point. I don't just eat my heart out; I chew the fat and gristle off of every bone. But somehow it doesn't work like that. See this…

(*Slapping her thighs.*)

Pure nihilism – it goes straight to my thighs.

(*Beat.*)

Every once in a while I'll take a little stab at a sort of resigned acceptance, but it doesn't usually last very long. Something really stupid happens and I'm back at the altar of self-loathing. For instance, every so often I'll pass by a shop window and see an outfit that strikes me as divine – simply that. It is art – art to wear. As superficial as that may sound in this fucked up, hypocritical world, I'll sometimes see something so sartorially perfect in and of itself that all I can do is marvel. Then, as I'm marveling and admiring, my eyes gradually refocus onto something else, something quite different and much closer to me…my own image reflected in the window. And I'll stand there for a moment, trying to comprehend the duality of what I'm seeing. I try to reconcile the person I see in that pane of glass with the person who eyes and oh-so-adores and appreciates that…that perfect, stupid, perfectly stupid piece of perfection that's so completely beyond its reach.

(*Beat.*)

And that's about the sum of it, really – me looking enviously through a window; me eyeing stick figures in beautiful clothes, trying to avoid the middle image in the space between us – the one that's there now.

(*Beat.*)

And so I eat more than I should…to feel better than I can…and make it all so much worse than it is. It all feeds upon itself, you see. I cannibalize myself. Which again begs the question, why am I not thinner? And there's that voice again.

(In a masculine voice.)

"'Cause ya can't stop shovelin' food into that huge belly, ya greedy cow! Why don't ya get ya fuckin' jaw wired?"

(Beat.)

To which I ever so warmly reply, "Oh, just listen to you, you great big loveable lunk. Come on over here and let me give you a great big hug. Come on. Let me embrace thee, sour adversity, for wise men say it is the wisest course."

(Beat.)

That's William Shakespeare, hot stuff…What?…No, not Shatner – *Shakespeare.*

(Beat.)

He's not as bad as he sounds. If he spent as much time on giving his brain a workout as he does his biceps he might even be quite nice. As it is, he's destined to grow up to be his mother. And there's another fine example of the human race. She's one of those that always gives me "the look." I get a lot of people that give me "the look" – especially in restaurants. It's the look that says, "My God, she's so fat…why is she eating?"

(Pause.)

Another "fun" aspect of being massive, according to "The Bigger the Better," is being able to look beyond the physical attributes of those around you and appreciate the true beauty that exists within them. Your own abnormality, in effect, becomes a gift that grants you insight into the true nature of all of mankind, no matter how far removed they might be from the ideal. And that, quite frankly, is the most insulting suggestion of all in this worthless piece of dried pulp. How dare they suggest that I should give up my long-held and highly cultivated petty grievances against other members of society simply because I'm carrying around excess body fat!

Do they honestly believe that just because *I'm* stigmatized by society that I'm about to give up my own personal prejudices and start smiling benevolently and buy the world a fucking Coke? How ridiculous! It's one of the few things I still have in common with everyone around me. It's my last little bit of mainstream. And don't pretend you don't have them – we all do. We all have a little well of contempt inside us that we dip into every now and then – even the perfect people when they're having an off day. Sometimes it's just a way of surviving, because sometimes we all feel like miserable fat bastards in one way or another. Pointing a finger at someone else is sometimes the only solution to the feeling that you're the one at the bottom of the heap.

(*Beat.*)

André Gide once said, "There is no prejudice that the work of art does not finally overcome." And he may well be right. But all I can say is, that had better be one hell of a big canvas for someone like me because as it stands, I'm the last safe prejudice in society you can have a good old, side-splitting, roll in the aisles laugh at without feeling guilty. The day that laughter dies down…well, maybe then I'll begin seeing a little more inner beauty. When I see a little more outer empathy, perhaps then I'll have more of a mind to start blithely handing out cans of soda to complete strangers. Let's call it "The Coke Challenge."

(*Pause.*)

So, I've come to the conclusion that "The Bigger the Better," by generically named and instantly forgettable author, is nothing more than the self-justifying, gratuitous ramblings of some bored, bloated housewife who's married to some filthy-rich entrepreneur that's fucking every skinny brainless twink he can get his gnarled hands on. I've also a sneaking suspicion that part of her daily vitamin regimen consists of vitamin P – as in Prozac. I could be wrong, of course. It's just hunch.

(*Holding the book before her.*)

In short, as a self-help tool – not to mention a work of literature

– this amounts to little more than a trifle. In fact, that's not a bad idea. Yes...yes, I think I shall go now and buy a can of Reddi-wip and some squeezable butterscotch topping, spread it all over the pages of this book and eat it from cover to cover. This will be the first book that I can honestly say I have ever truly digested. And who knows, once it's inside me, being attacked and broken down by all my lazy little enzymes, maybe I finally *will* see the big picture.

(*Beat.*)

Don't hold your breath though.

(*Beat.*)

I shall leave you with a few words from Quentin Crisp: "In an expanding universe, time is on the side of the outcast. Those who once inhabited the suburbs of human contempt find that without changing their address they eventually live in the metropolis."

(*Beat.*)

So...perhaps I'll see you there.

(*Begins exiting R. then stops and turns. Then, to the tune of the song by Osvaldo Farres.*)

Perhaps, perhaps, perhaps!

(*PEGGY exits R. A second later the book is tossed back out onto the stage as the lights fade down to BLACK.*)

END OF PLAY

A SMALL ACT OF VANDALISM

A SMALL ACT OF VANDALISM

Malcolm, a gentle, middle-aged soul with a troubled mind, keeps his mother's remains sealed in a small porcelain box. What he keeps hidden among his memories, however, isn't so easily contained.

CHARACTER

MALCOLM: A gentle soul with a troubled mind. 30s-50s.

SETTING & TIME

SETTING: Unspecified.

TIME: The present.

A Small Act of Vandalism received its premiere production in London at the Off-West End Brockley Jack Studio Theatre in 2014, directed by Brigid Lohrey.

Malcolm......................................Daniel Brennan

An abridged version of the play received a staged reading at London's Royal Court Theatre in 2015.

At Rise: The lights come up to reveal MALCOLM sitting in front of a small table. Atop the table is a small, oval porcelain box. He stares affectionately at the box for a few moments before speaking.

MALCOLM: That's Mother, that is.
> (*Beat.*)

Well…not her in the strict sense, I suppose…just the bits and pieces of her left over from the cremation, you know. Sort of a dried and granulated version of her, if you will. A bit like instant coffee, you might say, only without the flavour. Not that I've…you know…I mean…good heavens.
> (*Beat.*)

That's Wedgwood, that is. Very expensive. Very expensive indeed. But worth it – worth every penny – 'cause Mother was worth it. Weren't you, Mother? She was. Worth every penny.
> (*Beat.*)

It's glued shut, actually. The lid, that is. I glued it myself with superglue – I had to. Seems criminal, really, doing something like that to a beautiful piece of genuine Wedgwood bone china. I'm sure if the Wedgwood's knew what I'd done they'd be all up in arms and fit to be tied. But it had to be done. Even so, I was riddled with guilt. As I squeezed the glue around the rim, I felt just like a vandal…like one of those yobs on the corner of Wentworth Street, with their saggy trousers and their big hoods with their nasty little eyes peering out…I felt just like one of them. But I had no choice. Not after the, um…well…the incident.
> (*Beat.*)

The thing is, I loved Mother, you see. I loved her ever so much. And when she passed on…well, I…it was, um…it was very hard. I missed her something terrible. Some days I'd…well, I won't get into that now.
> (*Pause.*)

Anyway…some days…evenings…when I missed her most, I'd sit

down and have a chat with her. Just me and her and a bottle of pale ale…having a chitchat. Well, I did most of the chatting. All of it, actually. But whatever I said, whatever I told her, I knew what she'd say in response, so it all made sense, you see. Anyway, I'd sit her down on the coffee table, take the lid off, open up a pale ale, light up a cigarette, and tell her all that was on my mind – just like before…before she…took her leave.

(*Beat.*)

In retrospect, I'm not entirely sure why I took the lid off to begin with. I think I thought she could probably hear me better, if that makes sense. Which I don't think it does. Perhaps it just made me feel a little closer to her. In any event, that's what I would do.

(*Beat.*)

But then, one evening…oh, about two or three months ago now, I suppose…I had…let's just say, one of my "off days." It had all become a little bit too much, you see. The images had returned. The final ones. You don't forget those. I try very hard, you see, to…to banish them. But sometimes they come back. And that day…they'd come back.

(*Beat.*)

At first I tried to hide it from her. I just chatted about this and that – general things, you know – like how I'd shrunk yet another cardigan in the wash, and that Mrs. Tottle at number twenty-three apparently had a new fancy man in her life, from what I could tell. But I knew. I knew that she knew. And I didn't want to talk about it…think about it. So I'd keep talking, and pour another pale ale, and have another cigarette…and another pale ale, and another cigarette…and another, and another…and I suppose it all started to get a bit carried away, and all these feelings started bubbling up out of nowhere, and just as I was telling her how angry I was with her, I saw myself flick the ash from my cigarette into her little Wedgwood resting place instead of the ashtray!

(*Beat.*)

I froze.

(Beat.)

Even though the room was sort of spinning around me, I froze. I was horrified. Mortified. How could I have done such a thing? To my own Mother? It was the ultimate slap in the face. And what could I do? I couldn't fish it out – it all looked the same. I could've scooped out the top part, I suppose…but some of that was Mother. I felt sick – sick to my stomach. But what could I do? What would you have done? I wanted to throw up. And then I went to the toilet and I did throw up. And I was glad I did, because afterwards I felt a bit better…a bit more…sensible. And I walked back into the living room, apologized to Mother very sincerely and without a scene, and vowed that the next morning I would seal the lid of her little Wedgwood tomb permanently and for all eternity – just like the ancient Pharaohs and Cleopatra, etcetera.

(Beat.)

So yes, even though in most respects this *is* my Mother, I suppose that, strictly speaking, I would have to say that this is 99.8% my Mother…and a tiny little bit of Marlboro Light.

(Beat.)

I did, for a moment, have this horrible thought that perhaps in introducing her to cigarettes, I might have inadvertently turned her into some pack-a-day fiend in the afterlife. But then reason soon returned. I mean, it wouldn't matter, would it? It's not as if everyone in heaven's jogging around in parks and taking vitamin supplements in the hope of squeezing out a few more years of it. You're just there.

(Pause.)

I often think I should scatter her somewhere. Somewhere nice and quiet and pretty, with birds singing. Just her alone with nature…and Philip Morris, I suppose.

(Beat.)

But then, where would I be? I'd be alone. With just my thoughts. And the memories. And the memories are good. Very good.

Wonderful. Just not the last ones. I can't be left with those. Not on my own.

(*Pause.*)

When I was a child, whenever I thought of death – which wasn't that often, don't get me wrong – I just thought you sort of fell asleep…forever. It wasn't something scary. It wasn't something you looked forward to, either. But it all seemed to have a nice, sleepy, peaceful veneer to it. But then, when I got older, I realized what a veneer actually was – not that I used the word at the time, it was just how it seemed – and I learned it was a thin, fake covering, not something real at all. I realized it was a façade…a word which came some time later. And then, even later in life – in more recent life – I realized that death can actually be quite horrible, even for nice people. I don't like to say it, but it's true…and it's best just to get it over with, because unless you're very lucky, there's not a lot of dignity in it. That's just a façade.

(*Pause.*)

I was never angry with Mother. Never. Not when she was alive. How could you be? She was just so lovely. Perhaps once or twice when I was very small. I don't remember, really. But that's normal, isn't it? I mean, kids are kids, aren't they? So it was…it was a bit of a shock to feel angry at her once she'd gone. Inappropriate, really. Not just because you're not supposed to speak ill of the dead – or think it, in my case – but…well, she couldn't defend herself, could she? And she had a defense…a very good one. But it doesn't stop me feeling angry.

(*Beat.*)

You see, before she died she asked something of me. Now, let me tell you in no uncertain terms that there's nothing in this world that I wouldn't do for my mother. Nothing. I'd have given up my own life for her at the drop of a hat…which in some ways, I think I might have done. But this…what she asked…well, it…it stretched the limits…of my love.

(*Beat.*)

But I did it anyway. And I'm still paying the price.

(*Pause.*)

Mother was very ill, you see. Very ill indeed. She had…well, something I neither remember nor found pronounceable to begin with. But whatever it was, was causing her system to atrophy. It was neurological, that much I can tell you. And progressive. It wasn't going to stop. First she'd lose her balance – would fall over for no reason at all. I'd pick her up, dust her off, and send her on her way again – just like a little wind-up toy. Then later on, all her coordination went to pot. Just picking up her teacup became something of a challenge. But we got through it. We found a way. For a while.

(*Beat.*)

And then…swallowing.

(*Beat.*)

Not something you ever think about, really. I mean, it's just automatic, so you don't. But if your body starts to stop doing it…well, then you do. And it became harder and harder for her to do it. It was all shutting down.

(*Beat.*)

And the next step…was breathing.

(*Beat.*)

And without aid…without artificial assistance…her body was going to forget how to breathe. And she knew it, and I knew it. They'd told us. But…while she still could…while she still had the chance to make a choice…she asked me to stop it. Stop it all.

(*Beat.*)

It was my mother. She was facing the unthinkable. And so I agreed. I loved her, you see. I'd have done anything for her. And I did.

(*Pause.*)

It was a simple plan. I was to take one of her favourite cushions – one she'd embroidered herself as a girl, when her head were full of thoughts of what lay ahead – and I was to hold it gently against

her weakened face until what little life left in her was
extinguished.

(*Beat.*)

And I was a good son. I did what she asked. What she
needed…so desperately. And I made her feel better. And I'm
glad of that. I try to focus on that. But I'm not always very
successful at it, to tell you the truth.

(*Beat.*)

Because now she's gone…and resting in peace. Hopefully. But
me…I'm still here. And however you want to look at it and no
matter how you word it…I killed my mother. I killed her. And I
love her so much, and I'm so angry at her. So angry, you wouldn't
believe. But it's not her fault. She's not to blame. And neither am
I…but I'm still angry. Because I hate life now. I can hardly live
with myself. I'm hardly living.

(*Pause.*)

I thought for a while I'd be sent to prison. I felt for certain they'd
figure out what I'd done and cart me off to prison and lock me
up with some of those yobs from Wentworth Street, with their
nasty little eyes. But they didn't. They never figured it out. Nature
of the illness, I suppose. I got lucky.

(*Beat.*)

Yes, indeed…what a lucky boy.

(*Looking down at the box.*)

Look at her, bless her – she has no idea. She's somewhere else
now…being lovely and kind to…some other people. Don't get
me wrong, I'm glad she's in peace…I just wish I was. And if I
had to do it all again, I would. I'd do it in a heartbeat…because it
was the right thing to do. She was owed it. Someone as lovely as
she was shouldn't ever have to suffer. I just wish…I just wish it
wasn't me that had to do it. That's all.

(*Beat.*)

And I get by, you know, like you do. I have my good days and my
bad ones. You make the best of it. But on the bad days…the days

I get angry…angry with Mother…who's the last person anyone should be angry with…that's when it's hard. I get angry with her for getting ill, you see. That doesn't make any sense, does it? But I do. I get angry and frustrated with her – as if she let me down. I start thinking of how it used to be, and how perfect it all was, and how she went and ruined it all by getting sick. Makes no sense…but that's what I do. Because as bad as it got, she was still there…until I made her not there.

(*Pause.*)

And I think…I think the worst part of all…is I can't talk to anyone about it. About how it makes me feel. It plays on your mind, you see – having to do something like that to your own mother. And it gets very hard sometimes. Very hard. But I can't. Can't say a word. Not to no one. 'Cause I'd be in ever so much trouble. Terrible trouble. So I just have to…you know…keep a lid on it.

(*He forces a half-smile as the lights fade down to BLACK.*)

END OF PLAY

THE REPLICA

THE REPLICA

An abused wife reflects on her past and deconstructs the emergence of the replica that now haunts her present.

CHARACTER

WOMAN: Stoic, contemplative, with a noticeably sardonic edge. Mid 30s-40s.

SETTING & TIME

SETTING: A dark room illuminated by a single spotlight.

TIME: The present.

The Replica premiered in Montréal at the Théâtre Sainte-Catherine in 2006, produced by Unwashed Grape Productions and directed by Paul Hawkins.

Woman..Laura Mitchell

At Rise: A light comes up centre-stage, revealing a woman sitting in a chair staring out ahead. She is dressed simply, her hair and face unembellished. She speaks in a somewhat detached, observational manner.

WOMAN: When I got up this morning the first thing I did was use the bathroom, just as always. Afterwards, as I washed my hands in a liquid soap scented with chamomile, I happened to glance up…and there it was, ever so sheepishly looking back at me. I wasn't shocked or surprised. It's there every morning. Sometimes I look at it, sometimes I don't. But it's always there…there in the mirror…the replica.

> *(Pause.)*

I'm not exactly sure when I first started seeing it. It wasn't as if it appeared overnight. It took shape gradually, over time. But I couldn't tell you when it began. When I see it now it almost feels as though it's always been there. But it hasn't. That's what makes it hard to look at.

> *(Beat.)*

I think the earliest I can recall it beginning to take shape was about four years after I'd married Karl. Nothing too pronounced at first; nothing to set off any alarm bells. Just a slight stiffening around the mouth, the eyes ever so slightly less…curious. It's strange how these things creep up on you without you noticing. Until it's too late, of course.

> *(Pause.)*

I married Karl in a fit of existential panic, and, like most decisions made in a state of panic, it wasn't a particularly wise one. He was older and colder, and quite successful. He ran his heart, mind, and business with ruthless efficiency. Not to be outdone by anyone, his rivalrous nature sought supremacy in all things – all but a popularity contest, that is, shrewd enough as he was to know that that was one battle he had no hope of winning. The very fact that he didn't give a damn what those around him thought of him made him doubly despicable to those who were unfortunate enough to have the pleasure – including most of my family. Unburdened by the need to please, he was free to treat people in whatever way would best achieve his goals, however callous the method.

(*Beat.*)

Why, then, would I have married such an autocratic bully, I hear you ask. Ah, but that's a trick question, you see – because *I* didn't. Not the person you see now. Not the one I can barely stand to look at anymore. No…it was a very different person that married Karl, as she wandered through the woods with her little basket, on her way to granny's house.

(*Beat.*)

She was…well, she was many things, but most of all she was lonely. Lonely and unloved. Yes, I know, I can almost hear the strains of a violin in the background myself, adding its cloying accompaniment to those hackneyed words. How pathetic it sounds now – especially now. And how ironic that the emptiness I felt then took me firmly by the hand and led me to this hollow place I now dwell in.

(*Beat.*)

Back then, she was the middle child of middle-class parents with middling expectations of her. They loved her, I suppose, as best they could. But in truth, they were both so busy resenting each other there was very little emotion left to go around. Rather than their child, she sometimes felt they regarded her as an all too real and unwelcome reminder of a time when they were once intimate.

(*Beat.*)

Nevertheless, despite their indifference, she'd decided she was destined for greatness and before long would be celebrated and adored the world over – as a novelist. First a bachelor's in English at a prestigious university, followed by her master's, then on to a hectic life of publisher's deadlines, endless book tours, interviews, children, more deadlines, more interviews, more children, holidays in far-flung corners of the earth in order to reclaim her sanity, then back to more of the same, and so on.

(*Pause.*)

When she met Karl she fell for him in an instant. Not because of anything he said or did – though he could be very charming when he wanted. No, it was his face that sealed her fate. It wasn't particularly attractive or handsome – not by accepted standards. But it almost broke her heart to look at it. It was so pitiful and forlorn – despairing, even. He had the sort of features that gave one the impression he was perpetually on the verge of tears. How could she resist? She wanted to make it all better.

(*With a sigh.*)

Ah, the treachery of images.

(*Pause.*)

She wasn't accepted into any of the colleges and universities she'd applied to, but higher education or no, she was determined that she would be a writer. Six months later, she'd completed her first novel and felt a level of pride and self-fulfillment that she's never imagined possible. After a flurry of rejection slips from all the publishers and agents she'd sent it out to, she felt decidedly less so. Still, unbowed, she continued to write, pouring her thoughts and feelings into her little worlds of love and longing.

(*Pause.*)

Sometimes I wake up in the middle of the night in great pain as Karl enters me from behind using a mouthful of spit and a great deal of force. Sometimes I have to bite the pillow to stop myself from crying out as he thrusts into me with increasing fury, muttering insults and abuse under his breath as he does so. It's not directed at me, I don't believe. It's directed at whoever he's imagining me to be at the time. I often wonder if it's always the same person or if it's someone new each time. Once, just as he was coming, I distinctly heard him say, "*Fuck you, Cohen, fuck you!*" I wondered if it was the same Cohen I thought it was.

(*Beat.*)

It hurts a lot…he's well-endowed. Sometimes I bleed.

(*Pause.*)

She began writing children's stories. After her second novel was rebuffed as unanimously as her first, she imagined this might provide a slightly easier route into the business. It didn't. Most of the comments she received referred to her lack of understanding of a child's imagination and of the somewhat trenchant tone of most of her tales. Clearly, the accumulation of rejection had taken its toll. It was around this time that she first met Karl.

(*Pause.*)

On a good day I'll ponder on what I might do to earn a living if I ever found the courage to leave here. On a bad day I'll think of nothing. Nothing at all. Hardly moving. Hardly breathing. Just being. And on a very bad day I'll sit and contemplate the number of pills I'd need to swallow in order to ensure success. My greatest fear is ending up as a vegetable – something not dead, but not alive either – and aware of it. Then again, degree or no degree, it may be just the role I'm most highly qualified for. I've made a few discreet inquiries on the matter from time to time, but there appear to be very few resources on the subject.

(*Pause.*)

A proposal of marriage finally brought an end to her roundelay of rejection. For the first few years things went relatively smoothly. Karl didn't want her to work, so she didn't. He made very good money – what was the point? She stopped writing, too, the impetus having abandoned her after the resounding thud of her initial efforts. About all she did do after a while was smile and nod at Karl's side at every party and business dinner he paraded her at. She wanted to get pregnant, but Karl said the timing was wrong for children. It would have been difficult anyway, as they rarely ever made love, and even then Karl always seemed to have trouble reaching orgasm. He told her he had a low libido. She believed him. It made her feel better.

(*Pause.*)

If I stare at it long enough – long enough to get beyond the taut features and the dull, expressionless eyes – I can sometimes make out faint traces of the original. They're small and hard to distinguish, but they're there – like little nail holes left in a wall by a former tenant. It pains me to see them. It hurts to be reminded of the original when all you have now is a worthless reproduction. How could I have squandered that so easily? How did I let it slip through my hands? Didn't I see it happening? Sometimes, I suppose. But it's all so gradual, isn't it? And then one day you look in the mirror and there it is. It's already happened. It's already too late. That's why most days I choose not to look. It's just easier.

(*Pause.*)

The success of Karl's various business ventures grew at an astonishing rate, as did his loathsomeness. Gradually, visits and phone calls from family and friends grew less frequent. She hardly saw Karl now, so busy was he making money and enemies. Her days became filled with television and tranquilizers – as prescribed by her general practitioner. She discovered that one seemed to compliment the other surprisingly well. She rarely went outside unless she had to. A quick trip to the supermarket or to get a prescription filled was all she could cope with. People always seemed to be looking at her strangely…as if they knew something she didn't. Once, the woman in the bakery told her she'd seen Karl late the other night stop his car and pick up a skinny blond boy a couple of streets away, and inquired if it was their son. She told the woman she must be mistaken, as they didn't have any children. The woman insisted it was Karl, and added that she'd seen him putting his arm around the boy, so obviously they were close. "Perhaps it was a nephew?" the woman suggested. "Perhaps it was," she replied. She stopped shopping there after that. She'd make do with sliced bread.

(*Pause.*)

Today being one of my better days, I'd been giving more thought to how I might support myself in the unlikely event I should ever regain consciousness. With a non-existent resume there would, on the surface, appear to be little option for anything that didn't involve washing dishes or scrubbing floors. I did, however, have an inspired idea this morning that might just provide me with a viable alternative to a life of low-paid drudgery – as a make-up artist. I don't know why I didn't think of it before. I'm actually quite good at it, and could be quite successful, I think, if given the opportunity. Perhaps I could work for a theatre company or in a television studio. I don't have any formal training in it, of course – I'm completely self-taught. I did buy a couple of books on stage make-up techniques, but otherwise it's all been a process of trial and error…and that's certainly no stranger to me. I've become quite adept at it, even if I do say it myself.

    (Pause.)

It got to the point where she'd let both herself and the house go to such an extent that even she couldn't stand it anymore. One morning, she got up and showered first thing, just like normal people did, made a little effort in her appearance – for what purpose, she wasn't quite sure, but she did it anyway – and began the task of reclaiming some sense of order out of the chaos that was now her habitat. With a zeal that surprised even her, she swept, dusted, cleaned, sorted, and organized. The bedroom, in particular, had become a shrine to neglect, and the piles of dirty clothes and discarded folderol seemed never-ending. Still, she persevered. Nearing the end of her task, she decided to make sense of the stack of business papers and printed e-mails that Karl routinely emptied from his briefcase onto the floor of his closet. As she stacked and tidied, she came upon a pornographic magazine filled with pictures of naked teenagers, all with Russian names. Dimitri, Vladimir, Igor, Kostya, Alek. She pushed the magazine back amongst the pile of papers as surreptitiously as she imagined Karl must've done on numerous occasions, and banished the thought of it from her mind. She'd never seen it.

(Pause.)

He'll be home soon…or perhaps not. Perhaps he'll be working late. If not, it'll be a grudging grunt of acknowledgement and precious little else…if I'm lucky. Two strangers cohabiting with absolutely nothing in common bar the fact that both found life to be a bitter disappointment, despite all the hype – albeit for different reasons.

Hardly a common bond, though, is it?

(Pause.)

The first time he hit her he seemed genuinely horrified at what he'd done. He appeared, in his anguish, and much to her surprise, to actually take a step back and re-examine himself and the person he'd become. The second time, less so. The third and thereafter it became a matter of routine.

(Beat.)

Like anything, I suppose, the more you do it the less you think about it. Familiarity breeds contempt…and contempt becomes familiar. It's all what you get used to, isn't it?

(Beat.)

Before long, she found her face to be hardening almost as fast as her heart. She thought about telling someone. She thought about a lot of things. It's all she ever seemed to do – stare out at nothing in particular…wondering if it would change.

(Pause.)

Lavender. I use lavender the most. Sometimes green, but mostly lavender. It's like magic. I can have the most unsightly yellowish-brown bruise on my face or my arm and with a little patience and a few brush strokes of lavender concealer beneath my foundation you'd never know it was there. It's a godsend. It's best to use a nylon brush, though, as natural hairs tend to soak up the concealer and not work as well. A yellow-based concealer works best for the eyes – black eyes, that is. It doesn't have quite the miraculous effect of the lavender, but at least you end up looking merely sleep-deprived rather than punched. The redder bruises require a more green-based concealer, which also seems to work rather well. When the situation calls for it, I can appear very colour-coordinated. Even Karl's impressed. I sometimes wonder who's the better concealer.

(*Pause.*)

On the night Karl was arrested she was watching "The Bridge on the River Kwai" on the television. As she sat contemplating Alec Guinness' blind commitment to a construction that could only serve to perpetuate his imprisonment, Karl was being finger-printed and having his picture taken. He'd been caught engaged in a sex act with a young man with a pierced lip in the men's room in one of the larger department stores. Mr. Buchenroth was summoned, conversations took place, smiles were exchanged, hands shaken, and nothing more was heard of it. As she'd reminded herself while sitting in Karl's brand new Porsche 924 just a few weeks earlier, it's amazing what money can buy. When the bridge finally exploded, tumbling down into the river, her sense of catharsis was palpable. Ah, the magic of the movies. She switched off the television and went to bed.

(*Pause.*)

I suppose I should do the same. No point in waiting up. A couple of pills and a sip of water and I'll soon be slipping off to that pleasant place of dark nothingness that has no facts waiting to be faced or eyes to be avoided. If I could, I'd sleep forever. In sleep I'm unassailable…unaccountable.

(*Beat.*)

I sometimes wonder – in more cogent moments – if that's not the reason I can hardly stand to look at it any longer…why I turn away when its tired, fraught gaze catches mine in the mirror. Not because of what it is, but for what it's become. Am I the one that did that? Is that my handiwork? In the grand scheme of things, am I the one ultimately responsible? By simply letting life happen to me, did I somehow become the unwitting architect of my own fate? Perhaps I did. That's not to let Karl off the hook. He has his own demons, it's true, and doubtless as many excuses as the rest of us, but at the end of the day it isn't the repressed hands of fate that blacken my body.

(*Pause.*)

But when I look back upon it all, a little part of me cannot help but think about all the times I seemed to let life simply wash over me, drifting along in whichever direction the current took me. It just seemed natural, somehow – easier. Why swim against the tide when you can lay back and drift? "Go with the flow," isn't that what they always say? Depends on which way it's flowing, though, doesn't it?

(*Beat.*)

Anyway…best not to think about it, I say. It only makes it worse. And the less you think about it, the less it hurts…and the better it all is. And the best part is, if I close my eyes…

(*Closing her eyes.*)

I can make it all go away.

(*The lights slowly fade to BLACK.*)

END OF PLAY

ONE NIGHT ONLY

ONE NIGHT ONLY

Denny, a prisoner on death row in a State Penitentiary, spends his final moments reviewing his career as a serial killer in an interview with himself.

CHARACTER

DENNY: A prison inmate on death row. Age open.

SETTING & TIME

SETTING: The execution chamber of a State Prison.

TIME: The present.

At Rise: A light comes up on a man, DENNY, dressed in orange prison overalls, strapped to a chair, downstage C. His arms and legs are secured to the chair by restraints. He addresses someone who is located behind a glass window beyond the fourth wall.

DENNY: Hey!

    (Pause.)

Hey!

    (Pause, then with ferocity.)

HEY!

    (Pause, then calmly.)

I know you can hear me. You're not so good at pretending, either…I saw ya flinch on the last one.

    (Beat.)

How thick d'ya figure that glass is then? Thick enough to stop me? Probably. Not so thick as to stop my voice gettin through, though, is it? Your little jump gave that away.

    (Beat.)

Come to think of it, this place is probably more miked and wired than a fuckin TV studio. Mike's everywhere, right? I bet even your name's Mike. No wonder you jumped. Bet my voice was *really* loud, eh? Mike?

    (Beat, then with a whisper.)

Can you hear me now?

    (Beat.)

How about that, eh? All this just for me. The lights, the microphones…my very own little stage on which to give the performance of a lifetime.

    (Beat.)

One night only, of course.

    (Adopting the voice of an interviewer.)

So, Denny, how exactly did you come to find yourself in your current circumstances?

    (Beat.)

Well, that's a very good question and I'm very glad you asked it. You see, Mike…can I call you Mike?…thank you…the thing is, Mike, I killed some people, you see…quite a number of people, as a matter of fact, and, well, you see, these other people found it, uh…how shall I put it?…*un-ac-cept-a-ble.*

(*Beat.*)

I see. That's fascinating. And how many people did you kill, exactly?

(*Beat.*)

Exactly? No one knows…except me. And I'm not telling.

(*Beat.*)

Ten? Fifteen?

(*Beat.*)

Sorry…that goes to the grave. Secret. We all have one or two we take with us, don't we?

(*Beat.*)

Yes, yes indeed. So tell me about the first time.

(*Beat.*)

The first time, the first time, yes, yes, yes…well, well, well…the first time, yes, well, I'd been thinking about it, you see – about killing someone – for quite some time. Quite some time. Years, as a matter of fact. And then one day I just decided to do it, just because I could, and…because I wanted to know what it felt like, and because I had the ability and the intellectual curiosity, and because…well, I think it's fairly safe to assume I was probably having a *bad day.*

(*Beat.*)

But you knew it was wrong, Denny?

(*Beat.*)

Wrong? What's wrong? It's only wrong if you choose to call it wrong. Same as right. Someone decides what's called wrong and what's called right. They just give it a name. They say that that's wrong and that's right, that's yours and that's mine. Doesn't mean they're right. It's just a choice. Look at him in there – he's about to kill me, and what's more he's being paid to do it by the same people who say what I did was wrong. So you tell me? And no one paid me. And I wouldn't say he looks particularly bothered about it either, would you? Look at him, shuffling around in there like he had all day.

(*Beat.*)

Hey!

(*Beat.*)

Hey!

(*Beat, then with ferocity.*)

HEY! I DON'T HAVE ALL DAY!

(*Pause.*)

So, Denny…what did it feel like…that first time?

(*Beat.*)

Oh, that's…that's hard to answer…hard to describe. There aren't words, you see? It's like…it's like the biggest rush you could ever imagine. Forget drugs and sex, this was…this was off the fuckin charts. In that moment, you're…you're everything. You're…you're God. There's this face, see…and it's disfigured with terror…and it's staring up at you, knowing its very existence, its very being, is in your hands…the same hands around its neck squeezing the life out of it. And you're God. And it knows it.

(*Beat.*)

But then…near the end, the face changes. The look of terror turns to awe…awe. I am the power. I am God. They see it. And finally, right before they slip away…the best part of all – and this was the same with all the girls, from the first to the last, the pretty and the ugly – they all looked the same at the very last moment. Just the same. Just before they slipped away there'd be this look of total innocence in their faces…like children…innocent little children…even the old ones. They'd look up at me with such…such innocence…like a child to a parent…not knowing what was happening to them or where they were going. Not knowing anything.

(*Beat.*)

And then they were gone…released…cleansed…at peace. I'd given them back their innocence, you see?

(*Pause.*)

Hey! I already told you I don't have all day. Why the fuck d'ya keep dickin around in there? Let's get this show on the road, buddy!

(*Beat.*)

Jesus H., you guys are pathetic, ya know that? Typical fuckin Government, makin a big song and dance over the simplest shit. It's not rocket science, ya know? You just stick the syringe into the vial, suck it up, step in here and do the dirty. I'll come in there and help if you like?

(*Beat.*)

I know what you're doing, don't think I don't. You're just dragging it out to fuck with me, aren't ya? I know the story – this is just what they did to Gary Gilmore. I read all about it. They kept putting it off and putting it off, when all he wanted to do was get it over with. Two stays of execution they gave him, and both times he tried to top himself when they did.

(*Beat.*)

Too bad. Don't scare me. Nothing scares me. Wanna know why?

(*With a smile.*)

'Cause Jesus loves me.

(*Beat.*)

Hey, d'ya know what his last words were before they shot him? Gary Gilmore? Do ya? "Let's do it." So come on, buddy…stop dickin around, let's do it.

(*Beat.*)

Hey, ya know what else? Guess who took his words and ran with 'em…literally. Nike. Yep, the good old sneaker people. Poor old Gary's "Let's do it" got their ad men all excited and inspired and they came up with "Just do it." True fact. Not exactly rocket science at work there either, was it? Still, it worked, I guess, and now those dying words inspire millions of sweaty little red-faced people all over the world to jog around their parks in the hope of living just a *little* bit longer.

(*Beat.*)

I don't think Gary would've approved.

(*Beat.*)

Denny, back to you…because, after all, tonight's all about you. So here's the big question: How did you get caught? When so many others don't, when so many seem able to slip back into society and never be held accountable…how come you were?

(*Beat.*)

Maybe I wanted to be caught.

(*Beat.*)

Like a…a cry for help? Wanting someone else to stop it because you couldn't?

(*Laughs.*)

Yeah, that's right. You got it. You're good you are, aren't you? Give me a fuckin break! I just got sloppy, that's all.

(*Beat.*)

Sloppy?

(*Beat.*)

Sloppy. *Slo-ppy*…comprende? Nothing unusual about that. We're all the same. You try something for the very first time and you want it to be perfect. You're sharp, focused, making sure every little detail's done right. But…as time goes on and you do the same thing over and over and over again, well…you get sloppy. You get lazy, you cut corners. The more routine it becomes, the more you lose focus. See, in the beginning I'd tape em up in trash bags – several of em, the thick ones, the garden ones. Then I'd drive at least half a day into the back country and bury em deep in the hills…deep, deep, where no one goes.

(*Beat.*)

But that's a lot of work. And like I said, I got lazy. I just started dumping em. Lazy and overconfident – that's where I fucked up. So let that be a lesson, kids.

49

(Beat.)

How much fuckin longer are you gonna be chokin your fuckin chicken in there? Hey…hey *FUCKHEAD!*

(Pause.)

So, Denny, in these final moments…no regrets? No remorse?

(Beat.)

Remorse? Serial killers can't feel remorse, you should know that? Someone hasn't done their homework very well, have they? Well, it's really quite simple. It's not that we don't…not that I'd want to…we just can't. Something to do with our frontal lobes, see? Read it somewhere. They're all fucked up. Can't feel it. Oh well…

(Pause.)

That said…there was one…one I regretted. The pregnant one.

(Beat.)

How was I to know? I don't have x-ray eyes. And that lying bitch didn't tell me. She didn't show. I didn't know. She should've told me!

(Beat.)

It was in the paper. Not good. You don't hurt kids. Not their fault. Nothing's their fault. They're just innocent…innocent little faces…'til someone takes it away…hurt's em…does stuff.

(Beat.)

No…ya don't hurt kids.

(Beat, then with ever increasing vehemence.)

But…when you're all grown up…well, you gotta take what's coming to ya, just like me, here and now, no fear, not me, don't feel nothin, nothin there, never was, never will be, just me, just me lookin at you, lookin at me, and I swear to God, if you don't quit jerkin me around and get out here now and get this over with, I'm gonna rip these fuckin straps off and come in there and make you wish you'd never been born! I'll rip that fuckin head off your neck and shove it through that fuckin window! I'll squeeze your fuckin eyeballs from their sockets and grind em into this goddamned floor with my bare fuckin feet, so help me God, I will! So help me God, I will! Now for Christ's sake, *JUST FUCKIN DO IT!*

(*BLACKOUT.*)

END OF PLAY

ORGAN FAILURE

ORGAN FAILURE

A woman in the viewing room of a funeral home addresses the body of her lover in the coffin before her.

CHARACTER

WOMAN: Attractive, with a strong and determined air.
           Sagacious with an acerbic edge. Age open.

SETTING & TIME

SETTING: The viewing room of a funeral home.

TIME: The present.

At Rise: The lights come up to reveal a woman standing before a coffin, observing the body that lies within.

WOMAN: Well, well, just take a look at you…all scrubbed and polished and ready for inspection. I have to hand it to them, they really did a good job on you. Who could imagine seeing you now that such a short time ago you were lying in a pool of your own vomit, your organs finally having decided to give up on you…just like everyone else.

(*Beat.*)

Except me.

(*Beat.*)

What did they stuff in your cheeks? Cotton, is it? Or some synthetic stuff? No, I think it's cotton…the look, the feel of cotton. Cotton mouth – how ironic. Well, whatever it is, it's a good look for you. You were always so gaunt and drawn, but now you look…well, quite lively. What a shame. Still, it'll make for a good send off. And like they say, you never get a second chance to make a last impression.

(*Beat.*)

I will miss you, you know that, don't you? Despite all those years of being second-best to…well, just about everything really: the wife; later, the ex-wife; the job; probably the dog…and oh, let's not forget the all-consuming, never-ending, neurotic bouts of introspection. If you'd been any more self-absorbed you'd have turned into a black hole. Just a small one, though. And last but not least, of course…the bottle. Though under the circumstance, I suppose that goes without saying. Yes, I think it's fair to say the only thing in your entire life you ever committed yourself to fully and unreservedly was the bottle. And look how it's thanked you.

(*Beat.*)

But, like I say, I will miss you. Because as awful as it is…was…it was what I knew. I knew it wasn't good, I knew I wanted better, but it was what I had…and I accepted it as such. There's a dealer in life, you know, and he's throwing the cards across the table, and the person next to you gets an ace and you get tossed a five of diamonds, and you think to yourself, well, that's the breaks. And you don't have to blame yourself for what happens, because you can blame it on the dealer. It's an easy out. And I took it. I went along with it all, and as shitty as it got, I could always console myself with the knowledge that I wasn't to blame. And in my head I guess I made the dealer my enabler. Kind of like you and your liquor store clerk, I'd imagine. So yes, taking crap from you became a way of life. And like anything you get used to, once it's gone you miss it. Doesn't mean it was any good…it was just always there.

(*Beat.*)

But on the occasion of our last conversation…something changed. Not in you; certainly not in your voice. That was the same, slurred, barely comprehensible, self-pitying rambling I was oh so very used to. No, it was…in me. Something in me…somehow…heard you differently. The feeble, garbled plea for help was just the same. My response – dropping everything and rushing over – was just the same. But inside…inside of me…well, I guess one of my organs quit on you, too. I didn't feel a damn thing.

(*Beat.*)

You see, what you don't know is…you were still alive when I got there.

(*Beat.*)

I looked down at you, crumpled in a heap on the floor, battered and bruised from yet another bender session of flailing around blind drunk. You weren't conscious but you were breathing. And I thought to drag you to your bed and get you cleaned up a bit, just as always. But I didn't. I decided to sit in the chair and contemplate things – contemplate you. And the longer I stared at you, the farther away you seemed. After a while it was as if I was staring at someone else. Someone I didn't know. And then you began to vomit.

(*Beat.*)

Your body started jerking violently as the vomit forced its way out of your mouth and nose. But you were still unconscious and breathing it back in, your throat choking on the acid, gasping for breath. And I sat in that chair watching you drown...until finally the struggling stopped and everything was quiet and still. And I waited...waited until I was sure the peace was permanent...for both of us.

(*Beat.*)

Then I called for help...even though neither of us needed it. Because, you see, sometimes in life...well, you've just got to help yourself.

(*The lights fade to BLACK.*)

END OF PLAY

WYWH

WYWH

Eileen, a reclusive, middle-aged divorcee still haunted by the loss of her son, discovers a new life in the virtual world.

CHARACTER

EILEEN: A warm, friendly, and good-humored exterior that belies an inner grief. Reclusive but curious. 55-years-old.

SETTING & TIME

SETTING: A living room.

TIME: The present.

WYWH was first performed in a staged reading at First Stage in Los Angeles in 2006.

At Rise: The lights come up to reveal EILEEN, a middle-aged, homely-looking woman, seated in a comfortable chair, staring at the screen of a laptop computer that rests upon her thighs. After a moment, EILEEN closes the lid of the computer and looks up at the audience.

EILEEN: I have presence…can you tell? Can't you feel it oozing out of my every pore?

(With a chuckle.)

No, probably not. That's because I don't – not in that sense, in the charismatic sense. Never did, really; not in 55 years. Just ordinary, I suppose. Always have been. No one you'd notice…in particular. *But*, I do have *a* presence. A web presence, that is. There's another me floating around out there in the cosmos. It's a new and improved me that no one can see, they can only sense. It's another life and it's ever so much fun.

(Beat.)

My name's "Misti"…with an "I." That's to say, that's my alternative me's name, not the real me's name – my name. I wanted something with a bit of mystery to it, a bit of the unknown. And a touch of the poetic – a bit more poetic than "Eileen," at any rate.

(With a self-conscious laugh.)

And all right, yes, if I were being honest, maybe just a hint of the young and sexy, too. Well, why shouldn't I? It's a new me, I made it up – I can make it whatever I want it to be. Who's to know? No diets, no plastic surgeons, just re-label yourself and change a "Y" to an "I" and 30 years of your life can just disappear in an instant. It's a modern-day miracle!

(Beat.)

Sam's the one who got me into all this. Sam's my nephew. He's a big whiz in the computer industry from what he tells me. Does all sorts of programming and coding and…whatever else it is they do. He's one of the best, from all accounts. Anyway, he's the one that pushed me online, as it were. He said I needed "modernizing," which I had a good laugh over. "Sam," I said, "I'm a woman on the threshold of old age, not a 1970s prefab kitchen – there's not a lot you can do to change me at this stage in the game." "You'd be surprised," he said. And I was. Mind you, I will admit there were a few scenes and tantrums and one or two panic attacks along the way – not to mention the day I broke down in tears, sobbing that if I couldn't even set the toaster right to do dark brown instead of burned, how on earth was I going to communicate with 4 billion people across the globe, most of whom didn't speak English? But I got there…eventually.

(*Looking down at the computer.*)

I mastered this beast…this magic box.

(*Beat.*)

He's a very patient boy, our Sam. And persistent. "You never come and visit, you don't show up at family get-togethers, and you never call us, so maybe this way we can all get to hear from you a bit more often." "Yes, Sam," I said, "You have my word. From now on I'll let my fingers do the talking."

(*Beat.*)

I do love him. He reminds me of my Billy in some ways. Or at least…how I imagine Billy would be if he were still here.

(*Pause.*)

I have a boyfriend now – did I mention that already? Hard to imagine, isn't it, me at my age, after all these years, back on the dating scene again. But I am and I do. His name's "Rocky"…with a "Y." We've been seeing each other for almost six months now. *Six months.* That's quite a long time – or it seems like it. Though I should add, we've never actually used the words "boyfriend" or "girlfriend" in any formal sense. It's more of an unspoken thing, really. But he makes his intentions clear enough. Once he sent me an instant message with an emoticon of a very stiff, expressionless couple holding hands, and underneath it he'd written: "This is us."

(*Beat.*)

I've been learning another language, too. There's no end to the challenges I'm taking on these days. Though this one still gets me a bit flummoxed at times, I have to confess. It's the language of the internet, and though it might seem simple in theory, it's actually quite tricky until you get the hang of it. I'm getting better, but Rocky says I'm still a WIT – that's Wordsmith In Training. I was LOL when I read that…that's Laughing Out Loud, in case you didn't know.

(*Beat.*)

If Billy were here he'd soon get me up to speed. He was ever so bright, he was. He took to books like a duck to water. Don't know where he got it from. Not from me or George, that's for certain. But he had a real head on his shoulders, did Billy. It was obvious to anyone. We had high hopes for that boy…high hopes.

(*Pause.*)

Anyway, I'm getting the hang of it, even if I do make the odd slip up, like last week when Rocky wrote and told me he'd just reached his one year anniversary of being clean and sober. He'd had a bit of a drinking problem in his past, apparently. Well, naturally I just felt so happy and thrilled for him, so I quickly typed back "So thrilled for you!!!," which I shorthanded as STFU – thinking he'd get my drift – followed by three exclamation points. Some time later a sad face appeared on my screen, followed by the words "Shut the fuck up???" question mark, question mark, question mark. Oh, I just felt so awful I could have died on the spot. It certainly taught me a lesson about making up your own shorthand. Go by the rules – the rules of the road. After I'd written back to explain what I'd meant he sent me back another emoticon of a big, beaming happy face that was wearing sunglasses, and next to it a pair of big red lips with the word "Muah" written beneath it, which he's already explained to me to be the sound you make when you blow someone a kiss. Like this…

(*Pursing her lips, she demonstrates making the sound.*)

Muah!

(*Beat.*)

It was ever so touching. Funny how you can feel so attached to someone who isn't really there, isn't it?

(*Pause.*)

Billy disappeared 26 years ago – almost to the day. He was 7-years-old and I was peeling potatoes. He came running into the kitchen asking for money for an ice cream. I told him he could take some from the jar on the counter and off he went, down to Mr. Hobson's on the corner, in his little yellow sweater with the hole under the arm that I never did get around to mending. And that was it…he was gone. He never did make it to Mr. Hobson's, according to Mr. Hobson. He just upped and disappeared…as if by magic.

(*Pause.*)

The first time I entered the chat room I was so frightened my legs were shaking – literally. Even though no one could actually see me, I was still overcome with nerves. For the longest time I didn't say anything – I just stood quietly in the corner, listening to all the different conversations that were going on. Well, reading really, but you know what I mean. But after a while I started to feel a bit more comfortable and eventually started chit-chatting with one or two of them. Just pleasantries, really – "Hello," "Where are you from?," that sort of thing. Nothing too in-depth. Anyway, it wasn't long before Rocky approached, greeting me with the letters HF." "What's that?," I asked. "Hello friend," he typed out in full. Before I knew it we were getting on like a house on fire.

(*Beat.*)

Just like a house on fire.

(*Pause.*)

They searched the neighbourhood with a fine-toothed comb, of course. Police, friends, neighbours – they all pitched in. It was all over the news, on the television, in the papers. Billy's face was everywhere…everywhere except back home. Someone had put his photograph on a flyer with a telephone number you could call if you had any information. That flyer was posted everywhere you looked. Every tree, every lamppost – you couldn't miss it. But then, as time went on, his story began to disappear from the news, the searches were finally called off, and the flyers became faded and torn and…blew away in the wind. Everyone moved on…everyone else, that is.

(*Beat.*)

A couple of years ago, as I was rummaging through an old drawer looking for what I couldn't tell you now, I came upon one of those old flyers. Gave me quite a start, it did. Suddenly there was Billy looking up at me…with that quizzical expression he sometimes had. I felt just like I'd been run through with a sword. I couldn't move. I just froze up, staring back at Billy's face and the four words in big, black print written underneath it that simply said, "Have you seen me?"

(*Pause.*)

About a month after Rocky and I met he asked if I'd send him a picture of myself, as he was curious to know what I looked like. This threw me into a bit of a panic, I don't mind telling you, as I'd…well, I'd…I may have said certain things to him regarding my age, looks, and body-type that weren't entirely accurate. But then I had a flash of inspiration. I decided that since "Misti" was my creation in the first place, I had every right to create her "look." So I Googled a few images of other people's family snapshots until I came upon an attractive young woman that seemed just right. She was sitting at a table, her head gently resting against her hand, with a pretty, sweet smile that just seemed so warm and inviting. "*That* is Misti," I said to myself. After I'd sent it to him I anxiously awaited his response. And waited…and waited. This was not like him. His normal response time was far, far quicker than this. Something was wrong. I suddenly felt very self-conscious. Was my Misti so very different than the one he'd been imagining? Was I not his type? Should I have sent a picture that showed more skin? My Misti was wearing a turtleneck sweater, it's true, but it was a very nice one and went ever so well with her hair colouring. Still I waited.

(*Beat.*)

At long last his reply came through. With my heart in my mouth I read over what he had to say, the realization of my mistake and the cause of his trepidation soon becoming very apparent. He said I looked beautiful, far prettier than he'd ever imagined. He also said I looked like someone who was a truly loving, caring person. "But," he added, "and please don't take this as anything more than a casual observation, but I did happen to notice that the chair you're sitting in is a wheelchair."

(*Throwing her hands into the air in incredulity.*)

Why had I not seen this? Was I in that much of a hurry? "Oh, you fool," I thought to myself. "Not only that," he continued, "but I also happened to notice that through the doorway to the left of the picture you can see a staircase, and I happened to notice that the staircase is equipped with a stairlift, so I was just wondering – and again, it's nothing more than idle curiosity – but I just wondered if…well…are you a paraplegic?

(*Turning away in dismay.*)

What had I done? I'd ruined everything. Why had I not noticed these things? Why was he studying all these other details so meticulously instead of focusing upon me? Oh, it was all such a mess!

(*Beat.*)

I had to think fast. Fast and on my feet. I had to erase this image of me from his head ASAP before he started thinking of me differently. I wanted affection not charity. Anyway, after some quick but rigorous brainstorming, I wrote back to him with an explanation. "Dearest Rocky," I said, "I may not have told you this before, but I am in fact an avid and quite accomplished ice skater. The picture I sent you was taken about two years ago, shortly after my disastrous attempt at a triple axel/triple lutz combination which resulted in horrendous debilitating injuries to both my legs. I am happy to report, however, that after much physical therapy and the intervention of a higher power, I am now completely recovered and on any given Saturday afternoon can be found at our local ice rink flipping and looping as if there were no tomorrow.

(*Beat.*)

He sent back a happy face, a thumbs up sign, and the letter/number combination GR8 – Great. And that's exactly what I thought.

(*Pause.*)

I suppose I'd grown used to being alone – feeling it would always be just me. Seemed normal after a while. But now Rocky's changed all that, of course. Changed everything, really. When George left I didn't blame him. It was a relief in some ways. The strain between us started to get unbearable after Billy had gone. We were never exactly a Hollywood romance to begin with. About the only thing we ever truly did share was the love of our son. Without him there it all became sort of exposed. It was just me and him again. And it wasn't enough. And I blamed myself, and he blamed…I don't know…me, himself, God, fate, everything. Truth is, I don't know. We never really talked about it much. Does that sound strange? Maybe it does, but it wasn't at the time. It had happened, we were powerless, and there was nothing to do except wait…and hope. What was there to say?

(*Pause.*)

Rocky wants us to meet. As it turns out, he only lives about 2 hours away by train. I'm giving it some thought. I already know what he looks like – he sent me his picture some time ago. And I know he doesn't look anything like Tom Cruise…or, more to the point, Sylvester Stallone. He's always been quite upfront about his age and looks and things like that. When I first opened the photograph he'd attached, I was not at all surprised to see a man of around 60 years of age, somewhat heavy-set, with most of his hair gone, and a kind but very weathered-looking face. And it looked absolutely beautiful…because it was absolutely real.

(*Beat.*)

Of course, if I ever did agree to meet I'd have to come clean about Misti. Though judging from one or two wry comments he's made in the past, I've a feeling he already has his suspicions. He's no fool, is Rocky.

(*Beat.*)

He doesn't know about Billy, but he knows I get sad sometimes. He's very supportive. When he doesn't hear from me for a while he knows it's because I'm going through what we call a BP – a Bad Patch.

(*Pause.*)

According to studies, the murder of an abducted child is a rare event, and of those that are, 74% are dead within 3 hours of the abduction. So, since no body was ever found, I know that Billy's still out there somewhere. And that's a comfort…some of the time.

(*Beat.*)

He'd be all grown up now, of course. Maybe even has a little 7-year-old of his own. Who knows? But I know he's there. I can feel it. I can feel his presence sometimes…out there…somewhere.

(*Beat.*)

I think he just got a bit confused, that's all. Got a bit distracted and confused and wandered off and got lost. And some nice family found him and took him indoors and made him something to eat and took care of him and…and when they found out what a lovely little boy he was they just couldn't bear to part with him. And I can't blame them really, because…because he *was* ever such a lovely boy. Who could ever bear to part with a lovely little thing like that? It would break your heart.

(*Pause.*)

I sent him an email yesterday. In the address line I just put "Billy." In the subject line I just wrote…WYWH – Wish You Were Here.

(Beat.)

A few minutes later it came back to me with a message from someone called "The Postmaster" saying, "Transmission failure. Addressee 'Billy' could not be found."

(With a nod of her head.)

Quite right.

(Looking upward.)

But I still think about you every single day, Billy – every single one of them. And don't ever think I don't, 'cause I do. 'Cause I still miss you just like it was yesterday. Just yesterday.

(Beat.)

WYWH, Billy.

(Beat.)

WYWH.

(Beat.)

Sad face.

(The lights slowly fade down to BLACK.)

END OF PLAY

ABOUT THE AUTHOR

From the Royal Court Theatre in London to the Playhouse Theatre in Tasmania, the works of award-winning playwright Andrew Biss have been performed across the globe, spanning four continents. His plays have won awards on both coasts of the U.S., critical acclaim in the U.K., and quickly became a perennial sight on Off-Broadway and Off-Off Broadway stages.

In London his plays have been performed at The Royal Court Theatre, Theatre503, Riverside Studios, The Union Theatre, The White Bear Theatre, The Brockley Jack Studio Theatre, Fractured Lines Theatre & Film at COG ARTSpace, and Ghost Dog Productions at The Horse & Stables.

In New York his plays have been produced at Theatre Row Studios, The Samuel French Off-Off-Broadway Festival, The Kraine Theater, The Red Room Theater, Times Square Arts Center, Manhattan Theatre Source, Mind The Gap Theatre, 3Graces Theatre Company, Emerging Artists Theatre, Curan Repertory Company, Pulse Ensemble Theatre, American Globe Theatre, The American Theater of Actors, and Chashama Theatres, among others.

His plays and monologues are published in numerous anthologies from trade publishers Bedford/St. Martin's, Smith & Kraus, Inc., Pioneer Drama Service, and Applause Theatre & Cinema Books.

Andrew is a graduate of the University of the Arts London, and a member of the Dramatists Guild of America, Inc.

For more information please visit his website at: andrewbiss.com

The End of the World

5M/3F Approx. 90 minutes

Valentine's parents have decided that the time has come at last for their son to make his own way in the world. Valentine, accustomed to a life of cosseted seclusion, isn't so keen on the idea. But go he must, and soon he finds himself venturing forth into the vast world beyond. His new adventure is soon drawn to a halt, however, when he is mugged at gunpoint. Frightened and exhausted, he seeks shelter at a bed and breakfast establishment run by the dour Mrs. Anna.

Here Valentine encounters a Bosnian woman with a hole where her stomach used to be, an American entrepreneur with a scheme to implant televisions into people's heads, and a Catholic priest who attempts to lure him down inside a kitchen sink. Then things start getting strange…

The Meta Plays

A collection of short comedic plays that take theatrical conventions on a metaphysical joyride.

This unique compilation of wittily inventive short comedies can be performed by as few as 4 actors or as many as 18, all with minimal set and prop requirements. Many of these plays have gone on to receive highly successful productions around the world, garnering glowing reviews along the way.

The Most Interesting Man in the Whole Wide World

1M/3F Approx. 90 minutes

Horatio Higgins recently lost his job. He also lost his parents, so he claims, though the precise cause of their demise remains something of an enigma. Living alone in his tiny flat, Horatio's sense of isolation is mitigated only by a near-continual dialogue with himself and by the companionship of what he affectionately describes as "my wife."

Things change, however, when he encounters a sweet, impressionable young woman named Nore. As their relationship lurches unsteadily forward, Horatio finds himself struggling against a riptide of conflicting realities that he is ill-equipped to cope with until events at last overtake him and a new yet oddly familiar reality emerges.

Leah's Gals

3M/5F Approx. 90 minutes

Leah's just won the lottery in what she describes as "the biggest single, one-time cash haul in this here dirt-poor, shitty state's history!" But, rather than living the highlife, Leah decides to split the winnings among her three daughters, asking only for a deathbed-style declaration of love in return. When her youngest daughter, Patina, scoffs at the idea, Leah disowns her with vitriolic fury. Bestowing instead the prize money upon her two eldest daughters, her dreams of a pampered retirement in the arms of her offspring for herself and her close companion, Pearl, seem guaranteed. Things soon turn sour, however, as long-held grievances and newfound wealth lead to familial treachery, violence and death.

Greed, lust, drugs, and Capodimonte combust in this low-rent, Southern fried twist on a literary classic.

Arcane Acts of Urban Renewal

Five One-Act Comedies Approx. 100 minutes

A collection of five thematically related, darkly humorous one-act plays in which ordinary people find themselves in the most extraordinary circumstances.

An Honest Mistake: Madge has long since surrendered herself to the verbal abuse doled out to her by her belligerent husband, Stan. On this particular evening, however, her fears of a rat beneath the floorboards, combined with her absent-mindedness, result in her dishing up Stan not only his evening meal - but also his just deserts!

A Familiar Face: Two elderly women, old friends, meet up in a London café shortly after one them - Dora - has been widowed. As Dora's grief and anger intensifies, her good friend Eydie begins to suspect there may be more to her angst than the loss of a loved one. When Dora calmly removes from her shopping bag a large glass jar containing a human head, discussions over its mysterious identity, and how it came to be lodged in the cupboard under her stairs, lead to some startling revelations.

A Slip of the Tongue: Miss Perkins, tired of the constant innuendos and sexual insinuations of her employer, Mr. Reams, has decided to hand in her notice. On this particular morning, however, Mr. Reams decides to take things one step further. Unfortunately, due to Miss Perkins' nervous disposition and a telephone that rings at a disturbingly high pitch, he soon discovers he's bitten off more than he can chew...or at least, one of them has.

An Embarrassing Odour: Ethel, a widowed pensioner, sits down one evening to tackle her daily crossword puzzle. Suddenly her tranquil world is turned upside down when a burglar enters her home, believing it to be unoccupied. As Ethel vainly attempts to forge a relationship with the violent delinquent before her, his concerns lie only with getting his hands on her valuables...that and the unpleasant smell that fills the room. What is that smell?

A Stunning Confession: During an evening in front of the television a staid married couple suddenly find themselves having to confront a new reality.

Suburban Redux

3M/1F or 2M/2F Approx. 90 minutes

After thirty years of arid matrimony and suburban monotony, Mrs. Pennington-South's only dream was that her son, Cuthbert, would break free of the cycle of upper-middle class inertia that had suffocated her. Raising him in the hope that he was homosexual, she soon begins dragging home potential suitors for tea – on this particular occasion a rather shy, awkward young man named Tristram. Cuthbert, however, finds he can no longer maintain his façade and at last confesses to his mother his guilty secret: his heterosexuality.

When Cuthbert leaves to meet Trixie, his new female friend, Mrs. Pennington-South – heartbroken but accepting – takes solace in the company of Tristram, and a mutual love of the arts soon leads to a new found friendship. After several weeks, however, Tristram's feelings take on more amorous overtones, and a confession of love for a woman almost thirty years his senior sends Mrs. Pennington-South into a state of emotional turmoil. Her anxiety is further heightened by the unexpected arrival of Cuthbert, merrily announcing that he has brought Trixie home for an introduction, and of the "big news" they wish to impart.

Mrs. Pennington-South, mortified at having to face the reality of her son's lifestyle choice, fearfully awaits the dreaded Trixie. Nothing, however, could have prepared her for what would come next.

Made in the USA
Columbia, SC
15 January 2023

10357478R00049